MUSIC BOOK COLOURING BOOK

Tip: Each design is on a separate page so that the color does not run

PINK

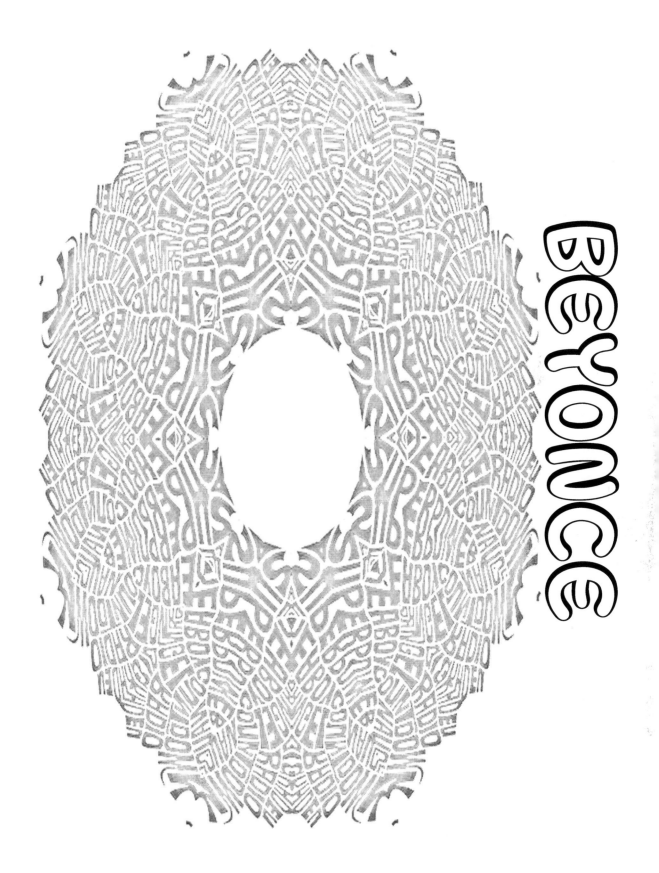

BEYONCE

Ed sheeran

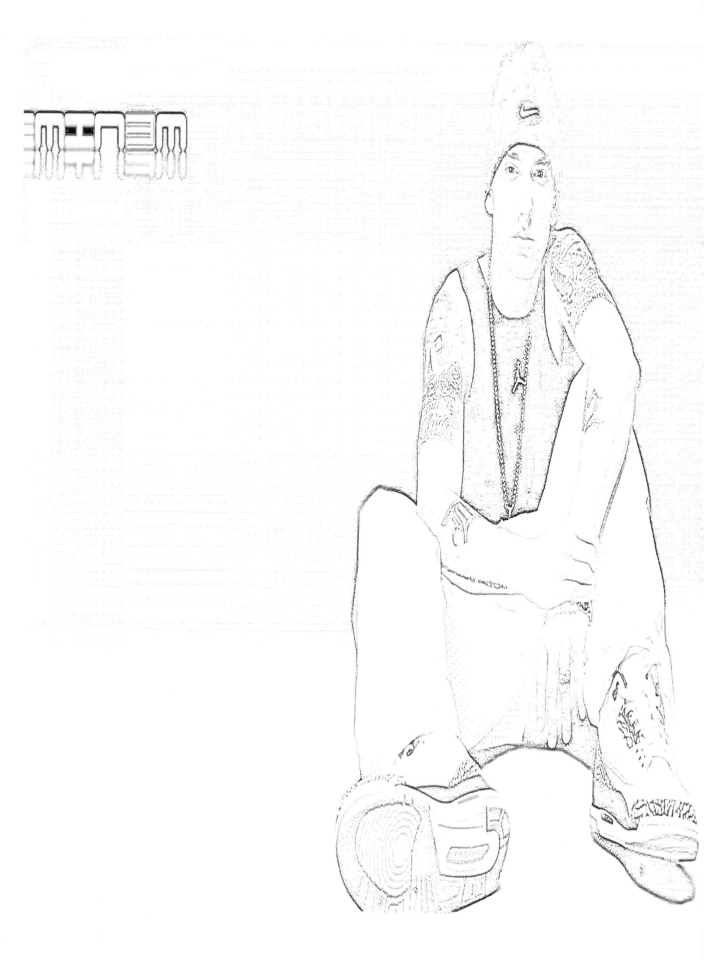

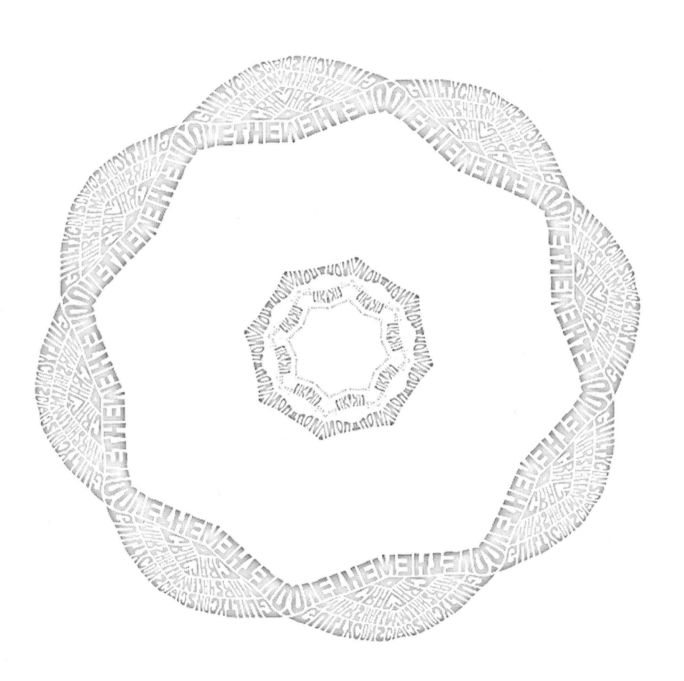

Justin
Timberlake

Katy Perry

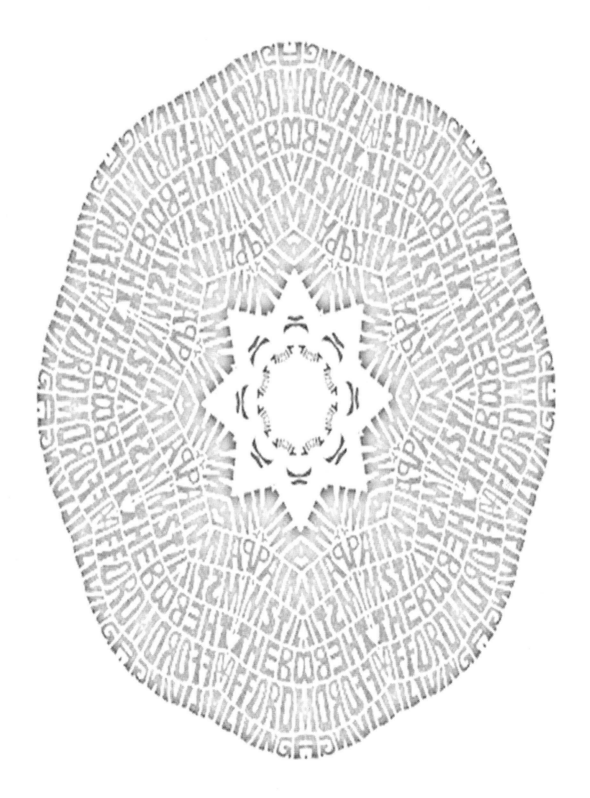

Lady
Gaga

Michael Jackson

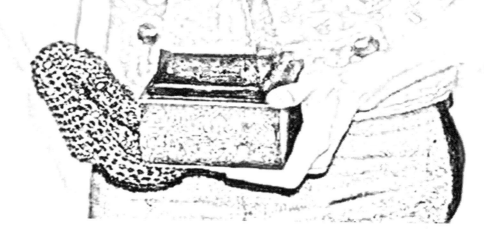

Rihanna

Sam Smith

Selena

Gomez

Taylor Swift

Made in the USA
Columbia, SC
01 June 2018